The Black Diamonds of
PROVENCE

Rob Waring, *Series Editor*

HEINLE
CENGAGE Learning

Australia • Brazil • Japan • Korea • Mexico • Singapore • Spain • United Kingdom • United States

Words to Know

This story takes place in the French region of Provence (prɔvɑ̱ns), in a town called Richerenches (ri:ʃərɑ̱:nʃ). It also talks about the Riviera, a holiday area in the southeast of France.

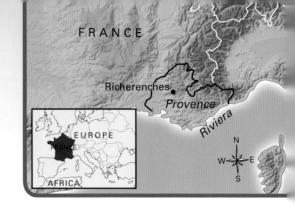

A **Truffles.** Read the paragraph. Then label the picture with the underlined words.

Grapes as well as lavender, a kind of flower, are grown in the rich farming area of Richerenches, France. However, it is the unusual and rare food known as truffles that has made the area famous. Truffles are commonly found under tree roots in the wooded areas near the village. Truffle hunters often work with different kinds of dogs, including yellow labradors, which use their noses to find underground truffles.

Hunting for Truffles

1. _____

2. _____

3. _____

B The Truffle Business. Read the paragraph. Then match each word or phrase with the correct definition.

Truffles are sometimes called 'black diamonds' because of their high price and rarity, yet they are still popular with gourmet cooks and eaters worldwide. The highest quality black truffles have small white veins in them and can be worth thousands of dollars. Therefore, the truffle business is very lucrative. Each winter many truffle hunters work with sniffer dogs to find truffles so they can sell them. Brokers then often sell the truffles to exporters, who send them to different countries. It's a cash business and most deals are done 'under the table' without paying taxes.

1. gourmet _____

2. vein _____

3. lucrative _____

4. sniffer dog _____

5. broker _____

6. under the table _____

a. a person who buys and sells things as a job

b. not legal; without telling the government

c. profitable or financially beneficial

d. a thin line

e. a person who knows about and enjoys fine food and drink

f. a dog that uses its sense of smell to find truffles

Black Diamonds (Truffles)   Real Diamonds

4. _____

In the small village of Richerenches, which is located in Provence, France, the villagers have gathered together in a local church. Each year at about the same time, they come to give thanks while they sing and pray to Saint Anthony. Why Saint Anthony? Because he is a special religious figure who is especially connected with truffles. These church members are actually praying to maximise the truffle harvest, and they are doing it at the region's yearly truffle **mass**.[1]

Truffle season is a particularly important time in the life of this village in the South of France. The little church is packed with people, and the **collection plate**[2] is filling up, but not just with cash. For the most part, people put money into collection plates, but something else is being put into the collection plates around here: truffles.

Around Richerenches, truffles are sometimes called 'black diamonds' because they are extremely rare and expensive. At a price of up to $1,000 U.S. per pound, they are one of the world's most expensive foods. Luckily for Richerenches, the relationship between these truffles and the village is a close one.

---

[1]**mass:** a church service
[2]**collection plate:** a dish used for collecting money for a church

The name Richerenches means 'rich earth.' It's an appropriate name for this village because the earth in this area of Provence is especially rich in truffles. Half of all of the black truffles found in France are transported through the market of the town, where they can generate up to $180,000 U.S. worth of business in just one day. This is definitely truffle country!

So just how important is Richerenches in the truffle business? It seems that it actually dominates the truffle market in France and is a key location for buying and selling. Truffle broker **Pierre-Andre Valayer**[3] explains, 'It's [a] most important market [for] truffles in France.' He then continues, 'So if you want to buy some truffles, you have to be in Richerenches to buy [some]. So for the sellers, it's the same thing. If you want to sell well, then you have to come to Richerenches.'

It's not surprising that the streets of Richerenches are packed with people buying and selling truffles. It's a diverse crowd, but they all have one thing in common: truffles. Everywhere one looks truffle brokers are talking to buyers, discussing the quality of the truffles, and trying to make a deal. They're all looking for truffles, and not just any truffle will do, either. The appropriate look, the richness of colour, the proper smell – all of these criteria must be met when choosing the very best truffles. But, of course, it's the delicious flavour that is the most unique aspect of this rare food, and the reason why everyone wants to buy it.

---

[3]**Pierre-Andre Valayer:** [pjer ɑndreɪ vɑlayeɪ]

Provence is not known for its fast **pace**[4] of life. In fact, it generally brings to mind summer holidays, lazy afternoons and ancient customs. The older men play traditional games like *boules* in the streets of the village, and life tends to be pleasantly slow. In winter though, it's truffle time, hence the small town's faster pace from November to March. Within a relatively brief period of time, the villagers often do a large amount of business in truffles – and the buying and selling happens quite rapidly. During this short interval, the small, quiet village of Richerenches comes alive.

Many of the region's local farmers also work as truffle hunters. After a successful truffle hunt, they then come to the marketplace in Richerenches to do business with France's truffle brokers. Most of the business is done discretely from the backs of the brokers' expensive black cars. The buyers smell the produce carefully in order to confirm that it's of the highest quality. Then, when the deal is done, the brokers weigh the truffles carefully and put them in plastic bags. Finally, money changes hands. One small bag of truffles is worth hundreds of U.S. dollars, so the trade is certainly lucrative, and the truffle traders here often make quite a killing.

---

[4]**pace:** speed

Infer Meaning

1. What does the phrase 'bring to mind' on page 8 mean? Look at the words around it and write a definition.

2. What does the phrase 'make a killing' on page 8 mean? Look at the words around it and write a definition.

Some say that truffle brokers use their money to live luxuriously on the Riviera.

Many people have opinions about how truffle brokers spend the revenue they earn from selling their 'black diamonds.' One truffle eater, for example, smiles and implies that he knows about what happens to the profits from all of those truffle sales. He suggests that the brokers buy property in exclusive **resorts**[5] on the coast and live a life of luxury during the off-season. He says, 'I do think they buy apartments and so on ... on the Riviera with this money.' He then adds with a laugh, 'I know that.'

It's hardly surprising that the truffle sellers can afford their expensive cars and apartments on the French Riviera. The buying and selling of truffles is mainly a cash business, and often it's under the table. This means that the brokers often don't pay any taxes on the money they earn and neither do the hunters. Deals are made in person, or at most on a mobile phone. Because of this, selling truffles in Richerenches is undoubtedly a good way to become – as the French say – *riche*.[6]

---

[5]**resort:** a relaxing place in which many people take holidays
[6]*riche:* the French word for 'rich'

Most people presume that truffles are an expensive luxury only for the rich; however, ordinary people who cook at home often spend money on them, too. That's because truffles have a unique taste which adds something very special to any type of cooking. Just a small amount of a truffle will enhance the flavour of an entire dish. When it comes to the flavour of truffles, there is no substitute. Because of their uniqueness, the demand for truffles is quite high while the supply is relatively low. This has resulted in the incredibly high prices for the product.

France's gourmet food companies also buy truffles from the brokers and, for a fee, will send most of what they purchase to other countries, like the United States and Japan. In truffle-exporter **Hervé Poron's**[7] company, employees carefully prepare the truffles for export. They weigh the local harvest and then select the best truffles before they clean them, and finally pack them for shipping. The best truffles are very black with white veins that run through them. The workers in Poron's company must carefully monitor the quality of the truffles and are experts at selecting prime truffles for export around the world; only a selection of the very best will please international gourmets.

---

[7]**Hervé Poron:** [erveɪ pɔrəʊn]

It seems that with all of this lucrative truffle business, Richerenches should have a bright and successful future. Unfortunately though, a potential problem may exist for the little town. These days, the truffle supply is declining; the precious black diamonds are becoming rarer. Poron takes a moment at the factory to discuss the disturbing situation. 'Today, if you find one hundred tons, it's a very good production. In fact, it's most of the time more like twenty, thirty, or fifty tons … compared to one thousand [tons], one hundred years ago.' So why are truffles becoming rarer? What are the circumstances surrounding the problem?

There could be a number of reasons for the decrease. One reason could be weather-related. If a truffle-growing area experiences a dry summer, it means that it will likely be a bad season for truffles that winter. However, the major reason fewer and fewer truffles are available is likely due to changes in the truffle growing environment. Poron explains the problem. 'To grow truffles you need woods, and the woods have disappeared,' he says, 'and what is left is not often very well taken care of … so we're desperate for woods. That explains the lower production today.'

The underlying problem here is simple: too many people are clearing truffle woodlands for farming and other activities and neglecting to care for the land that is left. Consequently, the decrease in the amount of wooded areas near Richerenches has probably been a significant factor in the reduction in truffle volume. Truffles grow underground, around tree roots. If there aren't as many trees left, there are fewer places for truffles to grow.

The countryside of Provence contains many large farms with broad fields. On most of their land, farmers **cultivate**[8] other **crops**[9] apart from truffles, including lavender as well as grapes for the famous regional **wines**.[10] With all of this cultivation of other crops, only a few places remain where truffles can still grow.

---

[8]**cultivate:** grow
[9]**crops:** plants grown by farmers for food
[10]**wine:** an alcoholic drink made from grapes

Predict

Answer the questions. Then check your answers on page 19.

1. What is the most important physical characteristic that a good sniffer dog must have?

2. What type of relationship must exist between a sniffer dog and its owner for the animal to be successful?

Despite the fact that there are fewer places left where truffles grow, there are plenty of people who are willing to hunt for them. Joel Barthelemy is one of those truffle hunters. He finds truffles with the help of one of his yellow labradors, Jade, a trained sniffer dog. Though all dogs have **sensitive**[11] noses, sniffer dogs are something special. They possess exceptionally sensitive noses and are specifically trained for locating truffles.

A good nose is one thing, but just how does a dog manage to find truffles that are hidden under the earth? Moreover, what motivates a truly good sniffer dog? According to Barthelemy, there are two different answers to these questions. As for how the dog does it, Barthelemy explains, 'The dog has to pay attention.' And as for the motive? That's a little more personal. 'He has to love his master,' reports the truffle hunter. 'You can do all the training you want, but the dog has to want to please his master.'

Jade seems to have the capacity for both of these requirements since she is certainly good at finding truffles. As the dog and her master walk through the woods, Jade puts her nose to the ground. Soon she stops and places her foot on a soft, earthy spot near a tree. This body language indicates that there are truffles beneath the soil. After Barthelemy harvests the truffles, he then gives Jade something nice to eat – a treat. As the dog and hunter continue their walk through the woods – and their search for truffles – it seems that, for today at least, there's no shortage of truffles. Perhaps Saint Anthony has listened to the prayers of the truffle hunters after all.

---

[11]**sensitive:** able to feel things in a stronger than normal way

After You Read

1. What does this story mainly discuss?
   A. eating rare truffles
   B. sniffer dogs and hunters
   C. the business of finding and selling truffles
   D. France's gourmet food

2. A good heading for page 4 is:
   A. Truffles in Provence
   B. Church Service for Truffles
   C. Collection Plate Season
   D. Saint Anthony Brings Truffles

3. Why are truffles known as black diamonds?
   A. Truffles are sold in black cars.
   B. Truffles are rare and sell for a high price.
   C. Truffles are dirty, but shine like diamonds.
   D. Truffles are difficult to sell.

4. Which characteristic is the main reason people want to buy truffles?
   A. the smell
   B. the colour
   C. the flavour
   D. the look

5. The pace of life in Provence is _____ in the summer and _____ in the winter.
   A. busy, lazy
   B. hot, cold
   C. slow, fast
   D. rapid, quiet

6. On page 7, why is the earth described as 'rich'?
   A. The people in Provence have apartments on the Riviera.
   B. Money can be found in the ground.
   C. People at the market drive expensive cars.
   D. Most of France's truffles come from this area.

7. The writer suggests that a cash business is a business that only
   _____ cash from customers.
   A. gives
   B. makes
   C. accepts
   D. produces

8. The number of truffles found in France is:
   A. declining
   B. increasing
   C. not changing
   D. difficult to say

9. What do the best quality truffles look like?
   A. light with no veins
   B. very dark with white veins
   C. very dark with no veins
   D. light with dark veins

10. What kind of summer weather is bad for growing truffles?
    A. no rain
    B. too cool
    C. too much rain
    D. too hot

11. Why are there fewer places to grow truffles now?
    A. because growing them is so expensive
    B. because people like wine and lavender
    C. because the growing environment is changing
    D. because sniffer dogs are difficult to train

12. Which of the following explains why Jade the dog is good at
    finding truffles?
    A. She is a sniffer dog and has a sensitive nose.
    B. Her owner is a truffle hunter.
    C. She likes to eat truffles.
    D. She is a yellow Labrador.

Truffle Farming

When you think about where truffles come from, you probably picture a small town in the south of France. While the French countryside does produce much of the world's supply of truffles, other areas are fast becoming important players in this lucrative game.

A DIFFICULT UNDERTAKING

The situation is clear: truffles can't be grown just anywhere. They must be grown near or under trees since scientists believe that this is what produces their distinctive flavour. It is also extremely difficult to cultivate them the way one would grow other crops. This special product doesn't appear in the spring and summer, but emerges only in the autumn and winter. Black truffles, which are the best-known of the French truffles, can be harvested only from November to March. White truffles appear only from September to early January. Furthermore, the weather conditions, such as the temperature, must be just right and the amount of rainfall must be adequate for the truffles to grow properly. Due to these challenges, very few farmers have mastered the skill of successfully planting and harvesting truffles on a regular basis.

TRUFFLES FROM ITALY

The world's second best-known supplier of truffles after France is Italy. The Piedmont region near the city of Alba is the centre of the Italian truffle business. There, truffles are sold in their original form and are also used in pastas, flavoured olive oils, and breads. Alba is best known for its white truffles, which many people feel have a finer and more interesting flavour than black truffles. Truffles are so important in Alba that there has been

Truffles are now grown in many countries around the world.

a truffle festival, which lasts for several weeks, every year since 1899. Thousands of truffle lovers arrive in Alba each autumn to enjoy the celebration and the scenery, and most importantly, to sample the truffles.

OTHER SOURCES OF TRUFFLES

Other countries, including Spain, Sweden, New Zealand, Australia, the U.K., and the U.S. also produce truffles. Currently Australian truffle growers are working hard to increase their share of the worldwide market. Scientists there have analysed the soils, rainfall levels, and types of trees available in order to maximise their production and produce the finest tasting truffles possible.

In certain parts of Australia, growing conditions are very close to those of the south of France and production is increasing year by year.

Word Count: 375
Time: _____

Vocabulary List

broker (3, 7, 8, 11, 12)
collection plate (4)
crop (16)
cultivate (16)
flavour (7, 12)
gourmet (3, 12)
lavender (2, 16)
lucrative (3, 8, 15)
mass (4)
pace (8)
resort (11)
riche (11)
sensitive (19)
sniffer dog (3, 17, 19)
tree root (2, 16)
truffle (2, 3, 4, 7, 8, 11, 12, 15, 16, 19)
under the table (3, 11)
vein (3, 12)
wine (16)
yellow labrador (2, 19)